Bibliotheca Mesopotamica

Primary sources and interpretive analyses for the study
of Mesopotamian civilization and its influences from
late prehistory to the end of the cuneiform tradition

Edited by Giorgio Buccellati

Volume Three

Inscriptions From Al-Hiba–Lagash

The First and Second Seasons

by Robert D. Biggs

Undena Publications
Malibu 1976

INSCRIPTIONS FROM AL-HIBA–LAGASH

THE FIRST AND SECOND SEASONS

SECOND PRINTING WITH ADDENDA

by

Robert D. Biggs

UNDENA PUBLICATIONS

MALIBU 1976

Second Printing with Addenda - March 1992

Library of Congress Card Number: 76-47770
ISBN: 0-89003-018-9 (hardbound)
0-89003-017-0 (paperbound)

Undena Publications, P.O. Box 97, Malibu, Ca. 90265
© 1978 by Undena Publications

To the memory of

MAURICE LAMBERT

1914 - 1979

TABLE OF CONTENTS

LIST OF ABBREVIATIONS

H   prefix for al-Hiba field numbers

H-T   prefix for al-Hiba field numbers recorded in a separate
                    catalogue of tablets (second season)

SAKI   F. Thureau-Dangin, *Die sumerischen und akkadischen
                    Königsinschriften,* Vorderasiatische Bibliothek, vol. 1
                    (Leipzig, 1907)

Sollberger, Corpus E. Sollberger, *Corpus des inscriptions "royales"
                    présargoniques de Lagaš* (Geneva, 1956)

PREFACE TO THE SECOND PRINTING

When the possibility arose of reprinting this volume, James Platt, the Managing Editor of Undena Publications, asked if I would like to update it with additional information and bibliographical references. It is a pleasure to do so.

This second printing is dedicated to the memory of Maurice Lambert who did so much to further third millennium cuneiform studies in general and Lagash studies in particular.

Chicago, March 1992   Robert D. Biggs

PREFACE TO THE FIRST PRINTING

This volume presents the epigraphical finds made at al-Hiba-Lagash in the first two seasons of the excavations conducted jointly by the Metropolitan Museum of Art, New York, and The Institute of Fine Arts, New York University. I am grateful to Vaughn E. Crawford and Donald P. Hansen, Project Director and Field Director, respectively, for inviting me to join the expedition as epigrapher.

With the exception of No. 3, an inscription of Enannatum I on an unbaked clay tablet (the actual text of which was to be inscribed on a votive object), the "royal" inscriptions were all inscribed on stone, copper, or baked clay. Many of the other texts on clay were not baked in antiquity. The heavy salination at al-Hiba means that many of them were damaged by the growth of salt crystals. These tablets were all baked at the site in a kiln constructed especially for that purpose. Most of the texts, with the exception of cone inscriptions, were copied in the field. My copies were collated with the originals in the Iraq Museum during a visit to Baghdad in the summer of 1972. A few fragments of cones and stone bowls were temporarily unavailable at that time, but in most instances I had both an expedition photograph and a cast, and these have been used to prepare the copies published here.

All copies are reproduced fifty percent larger than actual size. Measurements are in centimeters in the sequence height, width, thickness unless specified otherwise. All are maximum dimensions. Unless specified otherwise, the inscriptions are Pre-Sargonic and are written in Sumerian.

I am grateful to Dr. Isa Salman, Director General of Antiquities, for allowing me access to the texts in the Iraq Museum, and to Dr. Fauzi Rachid, Director of the Iraq Museum, and his staff for facilitating my work.

I wish to thank my colleagues Miguel Civil, I. J. Gelb, and Robert M. Whiting, Jr., for their advice and help with texts in this volume. I am particularly grateful to Robert Whiting for his help with the Old Babylonian texts. Finally, I wish to thank Giorgio Buccellati for agreeing to publish these texts in the series Bibliotheca Mesopotamica of which he is the editor.

Chicago, June 1976   Robert D. Biggs

INTRODUCTION

The texts in this volume all stem from finds made during the first two seasons of excavations at Tell al-Hiba by the expedition sponsored jointly by the Metropolitan Museum of Art, New York, and the Institute of Fine Arts, New York University. The inscriptions from the third season (1972-73) have already been published.[1]

Since the preliminary reports give information on the site as a whole and on the excavated areas, as well as on other artifacts, only those details need be given here which pertain to the inscriptional finds.[2]

Area A, the area where the temple oval was discovered, yielded numerous copies of a foundation inscription of Enannatum I (No. 1 in this volume) as well as a number of copper pegs representing Šul-utula, the god of the Lagash dynasty rulers.[3] The pegs were too corroded for the inscriptions to be completely legible, but they surely bore the same inscription or an abbreviated version of it. Other inscriptions from Area A included only some stone bowl fragments found together not far from the eastern wall of the temple oval.

Area B, in the higher central part of the mound more than a mile north of Area A, yielded primarily Old Babylonian materials.[4]

Area C included a large building, presumably administrative, in which a number of tablets, mostly unbaked, were found. Among the first finds in the building was a sherd from a large vessel inscribed with the name of either Eannatum or Enannatum (the first sign is missing). A considerable number of sealings on unbaked clay were found throughout the building. Some of the more interesting ones have been published.[5] The entire area of the building was much disturbed in ancient times with a great many pits and holes. A number of the texts come from such disturbed contexts, but others, including an important inscription of Enannatum I (No. 3 in this volume), were from stratified levels.

A number of clay cones and other inscriptions on baked clay were found on the surface of the mound. When they were found by expedition members, an indication of the area on the mound was recorded as the findspot. Others were turned in by workmen and no specific location could be recorded for them.

---

[1]Vaughn E. Crawford, "Lagash," *Iraq* 36 (1974): 29-35.

[2]Donald P. Hansen, "Al-Hiba, 1968-1969, A Preliminary Report," *Artibus Asiae* 32 (1970): 243-50 and 18 figs.; idem, "Al-Hiba, 1970-71, A Preliminary Report," *Artibus Asiae* 35 (1973): 62-70 and 26 figs. A general report on the first two seasons was given by Vaughn E. Crawford, "Excavations in the Swamps of Sumer," *Expedition* 14, No. 2 (1972): 12-20.

[3]The following is a list of the stone and copper foundation deposits (A and B indicate that both a stone and a statue were found; numbers without A and B indicate that the deposit consisted of the stone only): 1 H 111, 1 H 112A and B, 1 H 113A and B, 1 H 114A and B, 1 H 115A and B, 1 H 116, 1 H 117A and B, 1 H 118A and B, 1 H 119, 1 H 120A and B, 2 H 5A and B, 2 H 6A and B, 2 H 7, 2 H 8. It did not seem useful to give here the detailed information on loci and dimensions for individual objects. The location of the foundation deposits can be seen on the published plan (Hansen, *Artibus Asiae* 35, fig. 1). The deposit in the east wall of the temple oval (1 H 118A and B) was inadvertently omitted in this plan, but is shown in *Artibus Asiae* 32, fig. 1.

[4]See Hansen, *Artibus Asiae* 32, pp. 249-50.

[5]Hansen, *Artibus Asiae* 35, figs. 19-25.

Our inscriptions datable to specific rulers date from Eannatum,[6] Enannatum I, Entemena, Gudea,[7] Amar-Sin, and the Larsa Dynasty. Even leaving aside the foundation deposits in the temple oval, one has the impression of a great deal of activity at the site of al-Hiba during the reign of Enannatum I and probably during Entemena's reign as well. Nothing at all dating to the time of Uruinimgina (Urukagina) has been found. During the first two seasons, the only inscription of Gudea was the one mentioned above commemorating building activity in Nina-Sirara, but subsequently Gudea's work on the temple É-ba-gará has been documented through a number of baked bricks (part of the inscription had been known for a number of years).[8] The inscription of Amar-Sin is a well-known one and does not necessarily imply much activity at the site in the Ur III period.

It is probable that the Pre-Sargonic administrative texts date from the reigns of Enannatum I or Entemena. Only three (Nos. 10, 18, and 20) bear the typical year designations of Lagash-area texts, a long horizontal wedge crossed by slanting vertical wedges.

Two tablets (Nos. 24 and 25) can be dated palaeographically to the Sargonic era. One was found in an ancient cut and the other in fill not far below the present surface in a disturbed context.

The remainder of the tablets are Old Babylonian and are presented here as a group (Nos. 36-41). The contracts all have seal impressions. Regrettably, I have not been able to have adequate drawings made of them, but, because of the obvious interest in seal impressions on dated tablets, I have included photographs.

None of us who worked at the site of al-Hiba have seen evidence that the site was occupied after the Old Babylonian period. The recent suggestion of W. G. Lambert that al-Hiba — Lagash, which in Sumerian times had a quarter called Uru-kù, may be the site of the capital of the Sealand Dynasty[9] appears to me to be unlikely. Admittedly, one may eventually find first millennium artifacts in wells, drains, or pits, but any significant first millennium occupation anywhere on the site seems unlikely.

---

[6] Represented by a seal impression published in *Artibus Asiae* 35, fig. 19, and possibly by two small surface finds, for which see the descriptions of Nos. 6 and 7 below.

[7] One copy of the Gudea text (1 H 79) was found in the excavations, but out of context in an Old Babylonian level; another small fragment (2 H-T 16) was a surface find. I assume that it was not made at al-Hiba but was brought from Nina-Sirara in antiquity. It corresponds to Backstein H (SAKI, p. 142, No. v). My suggestion on the origin of it is based on the fact that this is a very common inscription at Surghul. On more texts from this site see below, pp.

[8] See Vaughn E. Crawford, "Lagash," *Iraq* 36 (1974): 29-32.

[9] W. G. Lambert, "The Home of the First Sealand Dynasty," *Journal of Cuneiform Studies* 26 (1974)[published 1976]: pp. 208-10.

DESCRIPTION OF AUTOGRAPHED TEXTS

No. 1

1 H 112A.   Area A, X 1111.75 Y 1148.48, just under the surface in the fourth course of bricks from the bottom of Level I platform.   Length 21.4, width 14, thickness 9.5   Foundation stone of Enannatum I for the Ibgal of Inanna, duplicate of Sollberger, Corpus, En. I 22, with the lacunae now filled.   Parts of several signs in the copy have been restored from duplicates.   The text is translated by E. Sollberger in E. Sollberger and J.-R Kupper, *Inscriptions royales sumériennes et akkadiennes* (Paris, 1971), p. 64.

Note that in a number of instances the engraver seems to have taken advantage of the vertical column rulings to supply some of the final vertical wedges in the signs.

No. 2

2 H-T 28.   Area C, E 200 balk between N 10 and N 20, room 18, cut in Level IA.   Length 9.9, diameter 6.3.   Cone of Enannatum I recording the building of the KIB by his official Šu-ni-al-dugud (who also appears in No. 10 in this volume).   In duplicates (e.g., 1 H 49) -ba is preserved at the end of the line in column ii 1.   This text differs from Sollberger, Corpus, En. I 10 only in the terms referring to Šu-ni-al-dugud in our text and to Lum-ma-tur in En. I 10.   Fragments not preserving these lines are therefore indistinguishable.

No. 3

2 H-T 21.   Area C, N 10-20, E 210 balk, room 4, southwest corner, in Level IB fill.   12 x 12 x 3. Dedicatory inscription of Enannatum I.   Published by R. D. Biggs, "Enannatum I of Lagash and Ur-lumma of Umma: A New Text," *Kramer Anniversary Volume*, Alter Orient und Altes Testament, vol. 25 (Neukirchen-Vluyn, 1976), pp. 33-40.

No. 4

1 H 88.   Surface in wadi east of Area B.   Length 8.4, diameter 3.3.   Fragment of a cone inscription of Enannatum I, duplicate of Sollberger, Corpus, En. I 10 (or No. 2 in this volume).   It is given here in copy because of the unusual feature of having the text repeated.   Note that the left column adds -na- where other texts have mu-dím-dím.

No. 5

1 H 3.   Surface in wadi south of the hill with the baked brick platform.   Length 6.6, diameter 4.4. Fragment of cone inscription, perhaps of Enannatum I, similar to Sollberger, Corpus, En. I 10 and No. 2 in this volume.

No. 6

1 H 11. Surface central area of the tell. 4.5 x 4.8. Small fragment of a baked clay vase, duplicate of Sollberger, Corpus, N 5. I owe to Maurice Lambert of the Musée du Louvre the information that he has joined N 5 to Sollberger, Corpus, Ean. 63. I am grateful to him for a detailed description of the fragments and photographs. There are traces of ends of lines of a column preceding the column designated i' by Sollberger, and one line is missing at the top of the column before É-an-na-túm-ra. The pieces join in such a way that the sign gír in N 5 ii 2 belongs in Ean. 63 ii 1 (actually line 2 of the rejoined pieces). M. Lambert believes, on the basis of color, lines in the interior left by the potter, thickness, and the spacing of the columns, that these rejoined fragments may be part of the same object as Sollberger, Corpus, Ent. 30 (erroneously described by Sollberger as a cone). If not parts of the same vase, they appear in any case to belong to the same text which existed in multiple copies.(The Tello fragments can thus be described as Ean. 63 + N 5 (+?) Ent. 30.) M. Lambert is of the opinion that these fragments are parts of an almost sperical vase approximately 11 or 12 centimeters in diameter with an opening at the top about the size of an index finger.

Note that No. 7 in this volume is a duplicate of Sollberger, Corpus, Ent. 30. I have not been able to verify whether or not Nos. 6 and 7 can be parts of the same vase, but to judge from the casts, they were written by different hands.

There seems to be no compelling reason to assign the inscription to Eannatum rather than to Enannatum I or Entemena and I leave the matter undecided for the present. I plan to publish elsewhere an edition incorporating the three Tello fragments and the two from al-Hiba.

No. 7

1 H 122. Surface. 6.1 x 5.5 x 1.9. Fragment of a vase, duplicate of Sollberger, Corpus, Ent. 30. See No. 6 for discussion.

No. 8

1 H 75. Surface near Area C. Length 5.7, diameter 3.8. Small cone fragment with dedicatory inscription.

No. 9

1 H 52. Surface. Diameter when intact 8, thickness 1.2-1.4. Fragment of a hollow cylinder (?) with parts of two lines of inscription, including part of a name beginning with Lugal. Unidentified. Not necessarily a royal inscription.

No. 10

2 H-T 12. Area C, N 30 balk in Level IB fill. 13.3 x 13.3 x 4.5. Contract on baked clay involving Lum-ma-tur, son of Enannatum I, for sale of land. To be edited by I. J. Gelb in his edition of "ancient kudurrus." Note that Šu-ni-al-dugud (column xi) appears as an official of Enannatum I in No. 2 in this volume, column ii 3.

No. 11

2 H-T 4. Area C, N 0-10, E 210-220, room 6, cut in Level IB floor. Fragment A: outer diameter about 8.5, diameter of hole about 3.5, width 4.8; Fragment B: width 1.8. Contract for sale of land. To be edited by I. J. Gelb in his edition of "ancient kudurrus." It is uncertain where fragment B should be placed in relation to A. The line numbers are those of Gelb's edition, which takes into account the number of lines estimated to be missing. The small area of the join in column ii 4 was only at the very surface and precluded gluing the fragments together to measure the amount missing. There are a number of impressions of string within the pieces; they seemed partially baked.

No. 12

2 H-T 2. Area C, N 0-10, E 200-210, room 18, Level I fill. 3.9 x 4.3 x 2.8. Upper right corner of an administrative tablet. The reverse is ruled in the middle, but the left half is broken off.

No. 13

2 H-T 18. Area C, N 30-40, E 200-210, room 44 in southwest corner on Level IB floor. 5.2 x 5 x 2.5. Administrative tablet concerning deliveries of reeds. Reverse uninscribed.

No. 14

2 H-T 29. Area C, N 30-40, E 190-200, cut in balk E 200 in Level IA fill. 16.5 x 8 x 2.5. Fragment of a large administrative text. Obverse entirely destroyed and covered by a layer of salt crystals.

No. 15

2 H-T 32. Area C, N 10-20, E 220-230, room 54, Level IA fill. 8.3 x 8.7 x 3.1. Baked administrative tablet (baked yellow like most of the material in the room) concerning oil, bread, onions, copper, garments, etc.

No. 16

2 H-T 24. Area C, N 30-40, E 220-230, east of room 52 or 79 in cut into Level IB. 5.3 x 5.1 x 2.6. Fragment of an administrative tablet involving grain. The reverse has only traces.

No. 17

2 H-T 10. Area C, N 0-10, E 210-220, room 7-18, on Level IA floor. 6.8 x 4.8 x 2. Fragment of an administrative tablet. The reverse is almost entirely destroyed.

No. 18

2 H-T 3. Area C, N 20-30, E 200-210, cut in Level IB from Level IA. 4.7 x 4.7 x 2.2. Baked tablet concerning cattle.

No. 19

2 H-T 1. Area C, N 0-10, E 210-220, room 2, Level IA fill. 4.9 x 4.7 x 2.4. Baked administrative tablet.

No. 20

2 H-T 20. Area C, N 0-10, E 230-240, room 70, Level IA fill. Diameter 2.9; length 3.7. Small egg-shaped pierced tag. For nam-dumu as a designation for a prince see Proto-Lu line 3.

No. 21

2 H-T 33. Area C, N 50-60, E 210-220, room 88, Level IB fill. 2.2 x 2.7 x 1.7. Fragment of a sealing (impression of the string is preserved) listing the contents of the receptacle as flour.

No. 22

2 H-T 23. Area C, N 30-40, E 200-210, room 42, on Level IB floor. 2.2 x 2.5 x 1.8. Approximately half of a small ball-shaped tablet, poorly written, probably a sealing (síg-babbar-gin, "ordinary quality white wool").

No. 23

2 H-T 26. Area C, N 0-10, E 220-230, Level IA fill near face of east wall. 4.2 x 4.2 x 1.8. Small round tablet with the name of the goddess Ninmah. Reverse uninscribed. The tablet is discolored as though from a latrine area.

No. 24

2 H-T 17. Area C, N 10-20, E 190-200, room 41, cut into Level IB. 4.7 x 4.1 x 1.8. Sargonic administrative tablet recording delivery of various commodities, principally fish.

No. 25

2 H-T 9. Area C, N 10-20, E 190-200, Level IA fill. 4.2 x 3.7 x 1.7. Small Sargonic administrative tablet.

No. 26

2 H-T 25. Area C, N 0-10, E 210-220, room 7-18, southeast corner on Level IA floor. 11.8 x 12 x 3.6 Riddles concerning cities. Published by R. D. Biggs, "Pre-Sargonic Riddles from Lagash," *Journal of Near Eastern Studies* 32 (1973): 26-33. Two small fragments from this tablet which do not join have been included.

No. 27

2 H-T 22. Area C, N 10-20, E 210 balk, room 4, southwest corner in Level IB fill, directly underneath, and partly smashed by, 2 H-T 21 (No. 3 in this volume), thus datable to the time of Enannatum I. 8 x 8.1 x 2.6. Literary text, closely related to No. 28 (2 H-T 5).

No. 28

2 H-T 5. Area C, N 0-10, E 200-210, room 18 on Level IA floor. 7.2 x 7.2 x 2.4. Literary text. Cf. No. 27.

No. 29

2 H-T 7. Area C, N 0-10, E 200-210, room 7-18 on Level IA floor. 10 x 8.8 x 3. Fragment of a text perhaps similar to the "spelling" texts published in A. Deimel, *Schultexte aus Fara, Die Inschriften von Fara,* vol. 2 (Leipzig, 1923), Nos. 62, 63, and 77. The reverse is badly damaged by a thick layer of tall salt crystals which passes through the tablet horizontally and comes to the surface on the lower reverse. A small fragment which may belong to this tablet has been included.

No. 30

2 H-T 8. Area C, N 0-10, E 200-210, room 7-18 on Level IA floor. 5 x 7.9 x 2.6. Upper left corner of a literary text concerned mostly with Enlil. The tablet is severely damaged by salt crystals, particularly on the reverse. It cannot be the same tablet as No. 31 (2 H-T 6). A small fragment which may be from this tablet has been included.

No. 31

2 H-T 6. Area C, N 0-10, E 210-220, room 7-18, southeast corner on Level IA floor. 6.6 x 5.2 x 3.3. Upper right corner of a literary text. The goddess Nin-girim is mentioned twice.

No. 32

1 H 97. Area A, X 1115, Y 1071.30, Level II fill, nested inside 1 H 98 and 1 H 99. Height 8.6, base diameter 12.5, thickness 0.6-0.9. Inscription on a veined alabaster bowl. It appears that the three inscribed votive bowls may have been gathered together, already broken and with parts missing, in an act of piety. Found within the temple oval, they were surely all dedicated to Inanna. This bowl was inscribed about two-thirds of the way around. The base of the vessel is preserved, but only one fragment from the rim.

No. 33

1 H 98. Same locus as No. 32, nested between 1 H 97 and 1 H 99. Height 4.2, rim 18, base diameter irregular 13.5-14, thickness 0.9. Votive inscription to Inanna on a veined alabaster bowl.

No. 34

1 H 99. Same locus as No. 32, with 1 H 97 and 98 nested inside it. Height 6.5, rim diameter 18, base diameter ca. 14, thickness 1. Part of a six-line votive inscription on a veined alabaster bowl with about half the rim missing.

No. 35

1 H 87. Area B, A 1020-1030, B 1030-1040, room 8, Level IV fill. 6.1 x 3 x 1.1. Part of a votive inscription, probably Pre-Sargonic, on a fragment of an alabaster vessel. The fragment is flat.

No. 36

1 H 136A. Area B, A 1020-1030, B 1040-1050, room 3, burial 1 H B 3, inside a pot (1 H 131) with 1 H 135 and 137. 7.5 x 4.7 x 2. This tablet, and the two found with it, form a small archive of a man named Bur-Sin who was apparently in the livestock business. Old Babylonian, written in Akkadian. Settlement of a claim against Bur-Sin who lost 100 sheep given to him for guarding (I have not been able to find a satisfactory reading for line 7). Note the following "Amorite" names: Ia-ah-PI-DINGIR (line 5), Ia-mu-ut-Li-im (line 14), and Ma-ah-nu-ub-DINGIR (line 19) among the witnesses. There is no oath formula on either the tablet or the case, but the tablet is dated by a year name mentioning a šu-nir emblem; the year name is perhaps a variant of that in No. 39B (1 H 137B). The following are the variants from the case (1 H 136B):

line 2	a-na na-ṣa-[r]i-im
line 6	written on two lines
lines 8 and 9 in reversed order	
line 11	li-bi Ku-du-ú-[du]
	[ᵈ EN.ZU -ra-b]i
	⌈ù⌉ [Ia-ah]-PI-DINGIR
line 13	omitted
line 14	Ia-mu-ut-Li-im followed by LÚ.NIM.MA.KI, "the Elamite"
line 21	-àm at end of line
line 25	The year name as preserved is copied below the text of the tablet.

There are three impressions of the same seal on the left edge of the tablet and on the case. See Plates I, II, figs. 1-3.

The pot in which the tablets were found can be seen in Hansen, *Artibus Asiae* 32, fig. 17.

No. 37

1 H 128. Area B, A 1020-1030, B 1020-1030, cut in Level I. 5.7 x 4.5 x 2.3. Fragment of an Old Babylonian letter in Akkadian. The reverse is destroyed except for a few signs.

No. 38

1 H 135A. Same locus as No. 36. 8.6 x 5.2 x 4. Contract in Akkadian for sale of cattle by Warad-Sin to Bur-Sin. Dated to the first year of Sin-iddinam. There are several seal impressions on the left edge. See plate II , fig 4. The case is uninscribed except for DUB Wa-ra-[ad ^{d}EN].ZU, "document (or: seal) of Warad-Sin." Note that the oath is by Nur-Adad and Sin-iddinam, but that the date formula is MU ^{d}EN.ZU-i-din-nam LUGAL. A photograph of the reverse of this text was published by Vaughn E. Crawford "Excavations in the Swamps of Sumer," *Expedition* 14, No. 2 (1972): 16, fig. 2.

No. 39A

1 H 137A. Same locus as No. 36. 4.6 x 3.8 x 1.5. Contract in Sumerian regarding eleven goats received by Bur-Sin. The tablet is dated only by the month, but the case (No. 39B) gives the year as well. There are seal impressions on the tablet and the case, probably showing a presentation scene (very indistinct). The inscription on the seal impressions reads ^{d}EN.ZU-iš-me-a-ni / DUMU Nu-úr-^{d}EN.ZU / arad ^{d}Nin-šubur.

No. 39B

1 H 137B. Same locus as No. 36. 6 x 5. Case around No. 39A. Though damaged, it gives both the oath and the year name. The oath is by Nur-Adad as king and by Sin-iddinam. The precise significance of this double oath is not obvious, though one can assume that it was used at the very end of Nur-Adad's reign or perhaps during a co-regency. The year name (with mention of a šu-nir emblem) is so far unattested in published documents. See the description of No. 36 for another year name mentioning a šu-nir emblem.

No. 40

1 H 127. Area B, 1020-1030, B 1030-1040, room 3, fill in Level III foundation, southeast corner. 6.4 x 4.2 x 2.5. Fragment of an Old Babylonian letter in Akkadian dealing with a house which has been "opened," apparently without authority, and a dispute concerning payment for a dividing wall.

No. 41

1 H 129. Area B, A 1016.55, B 1032.20, Level I fill. Diameter 6.3, thickness 2. Old Babylonian school exercise tablet; the rounded side is destroyed.

DESCRIPTION OF TEXTS NOT COPIED

No. 42

1 H 4. Surface of wadi just south of mound with baked brick platform. Length 6.1, diameter 4.6. Cone fragment, duplicate of Sollberger, Corpus, En. I 10, with lines i 7-9 partially preserved.

No. 43

1 H 49. Surface, same area as No. 42. Length 7, diameter 3.8. Cone fragment, duplicate of No. 2 ii lines 1-2 and 6-9, with only the ends of the lines preserved.

No. 44

1 H 51. Area B, surface, southeast part of trench A. 16 x 5.1 x 0.8. Potsherd, part of the curved wall of a large vessel, inscribed with the sign NIN. The sherd is reddish-brown ware with buff slip.

No. 45

1 H 55. Surface near Area B. Length 6.2, diameter 6. Cone fragment, duplicate Sollberger, Corpus, En. I 10, preserving a few signs of column i.

No. 46

1 H 64. Surface near Area B. The inscribed surface, roughly triangular, measures 7 x 8.9 x 8.1, thickness 5.4. Fragment of a greenish baked brick with part of a stamped inscription of Amar-Sin, duplicate of SAKI 196 b or c (Backstein B and C), lines 2-9.

No. 47

1 H 74. Surface near Area C. Length 6.8, diameter 6.2. Cone fragment, duplicate of Sollberger, Corpus, En. I 10. The first column is preserved.

No. 48

1 H 76. Surface near Area C. Length 5.8, diameter 3.4. Cone fragment, heavily abraded. The traces seem consistent with its being a duplicate of Sollberger, Corpus, Ent. 44 ii 4-9, though only the signs mu-na-tag can be read confidently.

No. 49

1 H 79. A 1020-1030, B 1040-1050. Level IIB floor. Length 6, diameter 4.5. Cone fragment with inscription of Gudea, duplicate of SAKI 142 v (Backstein H), preserving the last half of column i and the first half of column ii for all lines.

No. 50

1 H 101A and B. Surface. A: length 2.6, diameter 2.6; B: length 2.5, diameter 2.5. Two small cone fragments, duplicates of Sollberger, Corpus, En. I 10.

No. 51

1 H 126. Area B, A 1027.26, B 1042.58, Level III floor. 6.3 x 3.7 x 2. Poorly written and mostly obliterated tablet, perhaps a school exercise. Old Babylonian.

No. 52

2 H 63. Area C, N 10-20, E 210-220, room 12, Level IA. 17.7 x 13.2 x 1.2. Inscribed potsherd, reddish brown with burnished surface, bearing the name of either Eannatum or Enannatum (the first sign is missing). A photograph is published by Hansen, *Artibus Asiae* 35, fig. 11.

No. 53

2 H 381. Area C, N 30-40, E 190-200, room 89, IB fill. 5.9 x 4.2 x 1.6. Seal impression with an inscription of Eannatum. Published by Hansen, *Artibus Asiae* 35, p. 70 and fig. 19. A photograph of the sealing itself is published by Vaughn E. Crawford, *Expedition* 14, No. 2, p. 17, fig. 7.

No. 54

2 H-T 11. Surface. Length 6.2, diameter 3.8. Cone fragment, duplicate of No. 2, with parts of column ii 4-5 preserved.

No. 55

2 H-T 13. Surface near Area C. Length 6.7, diameter 4.5. Cone fragment, duplicate of Sollberger, Corpus, En. I 10, with the middle portion preserved.

No. 56

2 H-T 14. Area C, N 10-20, E 220-30, east of room 54, Level IA fill. Length 5.7, diameter 3.7. Cone fragment, duplicate of No. 2.

No. 57

2 H-T 15. Surface at about N 1100, E 30. Length 11.3, diameter 4. Cone fragment, duplicate of No.2.

No. 58

2 H-T 16. Surface, at about N 1100, E 30. Length 3.4, diameter 3.2. Small fragment of a cone of Gudea (?); it appears to be a duplicate of SAKI p. 142, text v.

No. 59

2 H-T 19. Area C, N 0-10, E 220-230, room 55, cut in Level IA. Length 5.9, diameter 5.1. Cone fragment of Entemena, duplicate of Sollberger, Corpus, Ent. 45. Column i is preserved (ki-ág-gá-ne-ne in line 6), and a few signs in column ii.

No. 60

2 H-T 27. Area C, N 40-50, E 210-220, room 81, Level IA fill. 4.4 x 3.7 x 2.1. Tablet with nine deep holes presumably made with a stylus, evenly spaced in three rows. Reverse blank.

No. 61

2 H-T 30. Area C, surface, near balk N 40. Length 7.7, diameter 5.3. Cone fragment, duplicate of No. 2 , preserving column i and one or two signs in each line of column ii.

No. 62

2 H-T 31. Area C, N 0-10, E 230-240, east side of room 61. 6.5 x 6.6 x 4. Irregularly shaped school tablet (?). There are four columns of jab marks made with a rectangular implement. The two halves of the tablet were separated sandwich-like by a layer of tall salt crystals 0.8 cm. thick. Reverse blank.

Texts from Surghul

On two very brief visits to the site of Surghul (visible from al-Hiba but difficult to get to because of the marshes between the sites), expedition members during the first two seasons collected the cone and stamped brick fragments they happened to see. I made molds of the originals, which were subsequently turned over to the Directorate General of Antiquities. Of the 18 pieces which I could identify, 16 are duplicates of Backstein H (4 are stamped bricks, 12 are cones). To complete the record of our chance finds, the other two inscriptions are given here as Nos. 63 and 64.

No. 63

Cone of Gudea, variant of Tonnagel A (SAKI, p. 142) (Thureau-Dangin was surely correct in questioning a Babylon or Warka origin for this text [SAKI p. 143, n. 5 f]). It reads:

1. ^dNin-d[ub]
2. lugal-a-ni
3. Gù-dé-a
4. PA.TE.[SI]
5. ŠIR.BUR.LA.K[I]
6. é-a-ni
7. mu-na-dù

No. 64

Fragment of a cone of Enannatum I, duplicate of the al-Hiba text No. 2 in this volume. The preserved signs are from column ii, given here with restorations:

[gal]-kinda
[nam-nu-bán]da é-[šà]-ga
[an-n]a-da[h]
[KIB] mu-[dím]-dím

ADDENDA TO THE SECOND PRINTING

I am aware of the following substantive reviews of this volume:

Joseph Bauer in *Bibliotheca Orientalis* 36 (1979): 45-46.

Marvin A. Powell in *Journal of the American Oriental Society* 99 (1979): 475-76.

Amedeo Alberti in *Orientalia* n.s. 50 (1981): 252-57.

D. O. Edzard in *Orientalische Literaturzeitung* 84 (1989): 665-66.

Readers should refer to these reviews for comments and suggestions on individual texts. Additional bibliography, insofar as it has come to my attention, is given here, by text number.

No. 1

New edition and translation by Horst Steible, *Die altsumerischen Bau- und Weihinschriften*, Teil 1, *Inschriften aus 'Lagaš'*, Freiburger altorientalische Studien, Vol. 5, Part 1 (Wiesbaden, 1982) [hereafter FAOS 5/1] pp. 208-10.

No. 2

New edition FAOS 5/1 pp. 202-3. Alberti, on pp. 252-56 of his review, discusses this inscription (and parallel in No. 4) in detail.

No. 3

Edited in FAOS 5/1 pp. 198-202. Annotated translation by Jerrold S. Cooper, *Sumerian and Akkadian Royal Inscriptions*, I, *Presargonic Inscriptions*, The American Oriental Society Translation Series (New Haven, 1986) pp. 47-48. See also Cooper, *Reconstructing History from Ancient Inscriptions: The Lagash-Umma Border Conflict*, Sources from the Ancient Near East, Vol. 2, fasc. 1 (Malibu, 1983), with translation of this text on p. 49. For the colophon of this text, see the discussion by Cooper, *Revue d'assyriologie* 76 (1982): 191.

No. 4

New edition FAOS 5/1 pp. 186-88.

No. 5

Edited in FAOS 5/1 p. 204.

No. 6

Edited, with Girsu parallels (reconstruction by C. Wilcke), in FAOS 5/1 pp. 175-78.

No. 7

Edited in FAOS 5/1 pp. 246-47.

No. 8

Edited in FAOS 5/1 p. 367.

No. 9

Edited in FAOS 5/1 p. 367.

No. 10

Edited by I. J. Gelb, Piotr Steinkeller, and Robert M. Whiting, Jr. in *Earliest Land Tenure Systems in the Near East: Ancient Kudurrus*, OIP 104 (Chicago, 1991), pp. 86-88. Powell, in his review (p. 475) observes that this is the earliest cuneiform document yet discovered that can be attributed to a specific year of a known ruler.

No. 11

Referred to by Gelb et al. on p. 190 as No. 145. It is not separately edited, but is taken into account on the charts on plates 131 and 135.

No. 16

In all likelihood, this fragment is Neo-Sumerian as suggested by J. Bauer, primarily on the basis of the personal name. The tablet was found in a cut from a later level and clearly is not contemporary with the building in which it was found.

No. 26

Bauer's review includes improved readings of several lines of these riddles. He gives a glossary of the composition (names of places, deities, fish names, etc.) in "Eine Wortliste zu IHL 26," *Altorientalische Notizen* No. 6 (1978). See also M. Civil, "Sumerian Riddles: A Corpus," *Aula Orientalis* 5 (1987): 17 and n. 1.

No. 27-28

Edited by Amedeo Alberti, "Due testi lessicali da Lagash presargonica?," *Rivista degli studi orientali* 44 (1980): 1-13.

No. 29

Edited by M. Civil, "An Early Dynastic School Exercise from Lagaš (Al-Hiba 29)," *Bibliotheca Orientalis* 40 (1983): 559-66, with collations.

No. 31

Identified as an incantation by G. Pettinato. See "Le Collezioni én-é-nu-ru di Ebla," *Oriens antiquus* 18 (1979): 329-51, especially p. 332 n. 25 and p. 347 No. 15.

No. 36

For the year names in these Old Babylonian texts, see M. Stol apud J. Bauer in his review.

No. 40

Most of this letter is translated by Edzard in his review cited above.

Nos. 49, 58, 63

These Gudea inscriptions are listed by W. Farber in his "Bibliographischer Schlüssel zu den von A. Falkenstein in AnOr. 28-30 verwendeten Siglen," in D. O. Edzard, W. Farber, and W. R. Mayer, *Ergänzungsheft zu A. Falkenstein, Grammatik der Sprache Gudeas von Lagaš*, Analecta Orientalia 29A (Rome, 1978), p. 65*.

No. 63

Not a variant of Gudea Tonnagel A, but a duplicate of Tonnagel I. See W. Farber, *Revue d'assyriologie* 72 (1978): 190-91.

CUNEIFORM COPIES

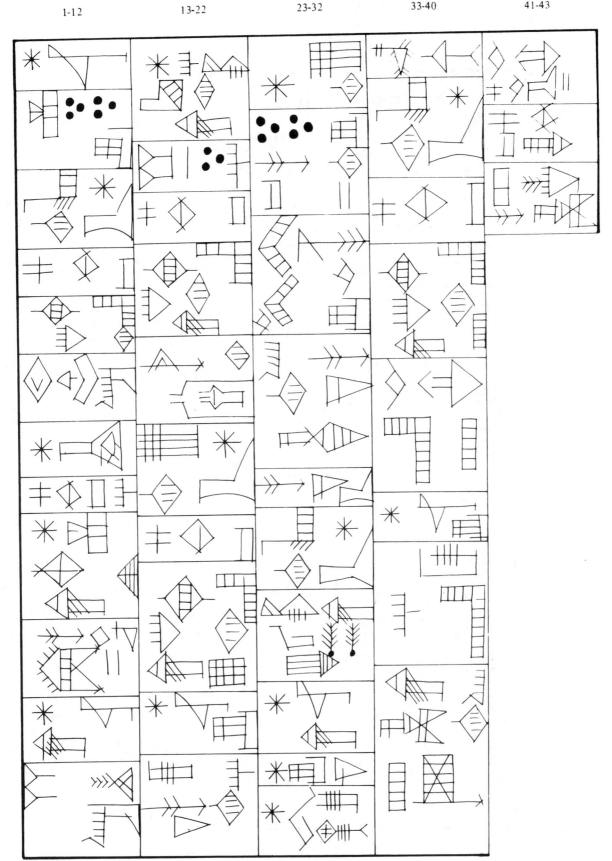

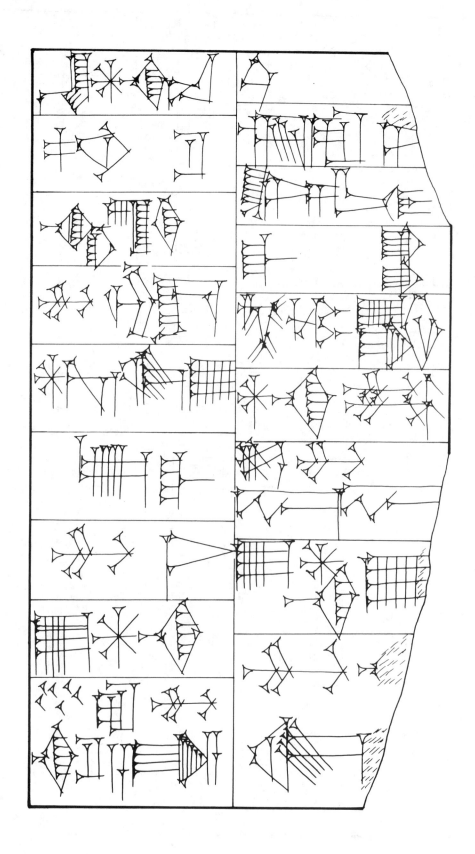

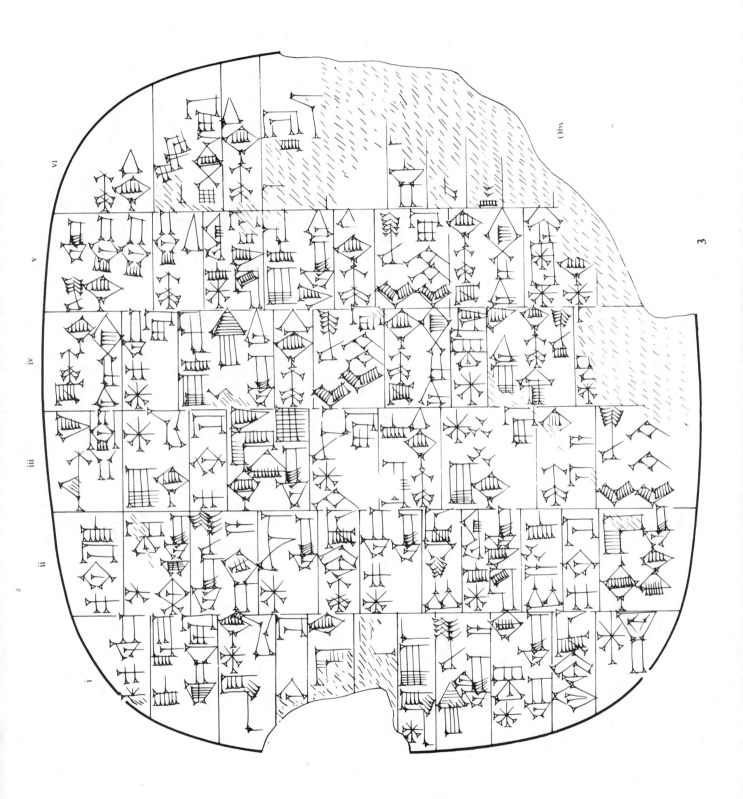

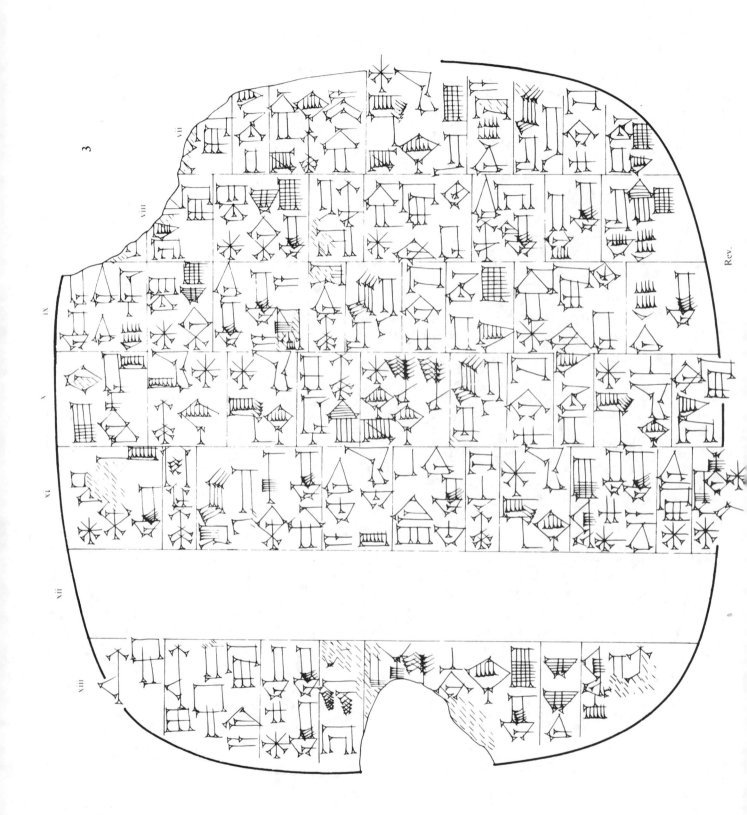

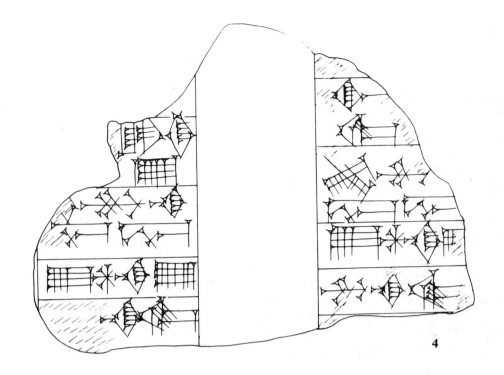

4

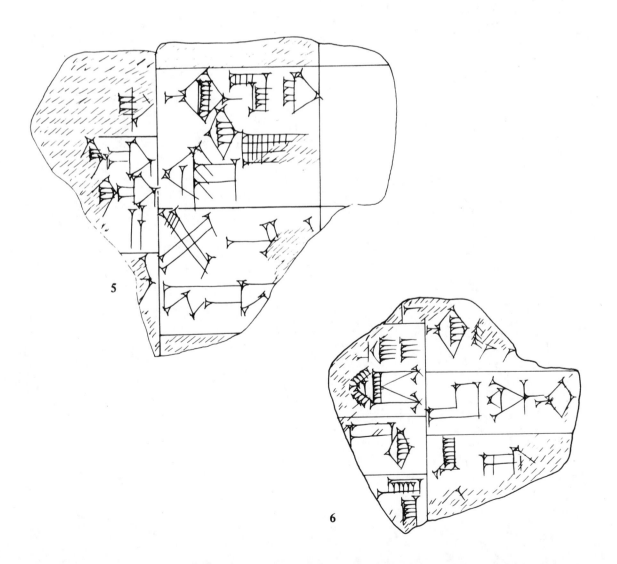

5

6

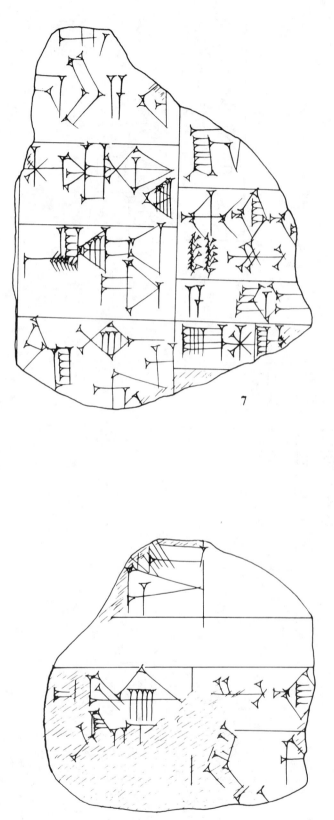

7

8

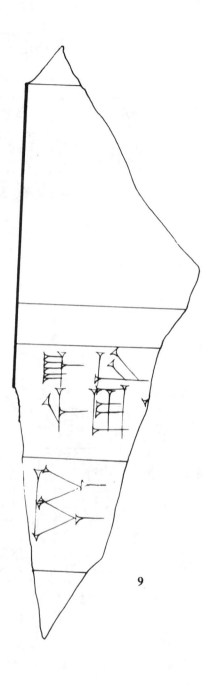

9

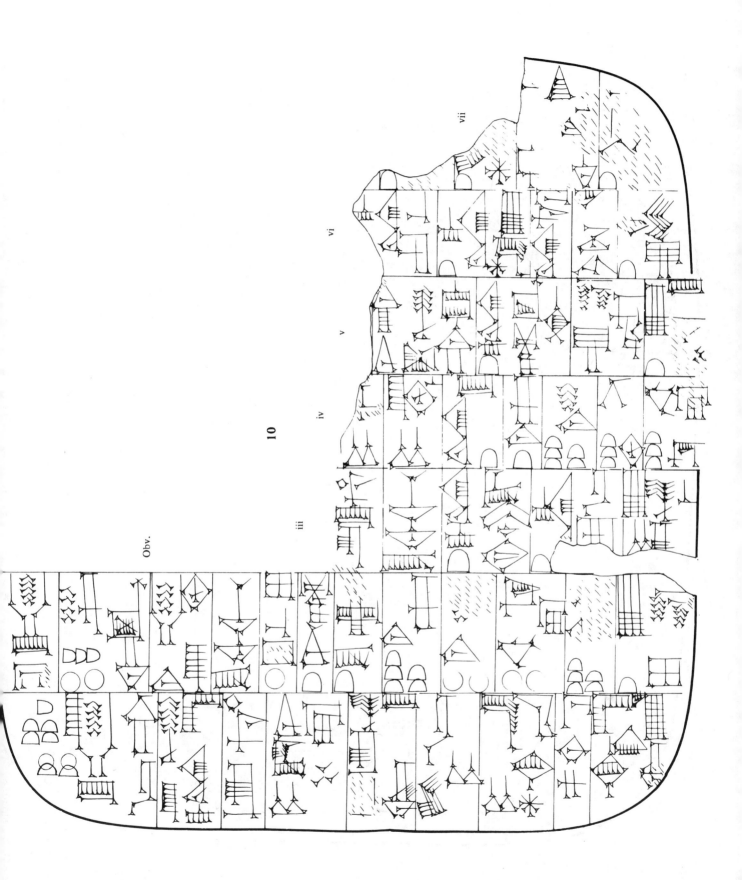

24

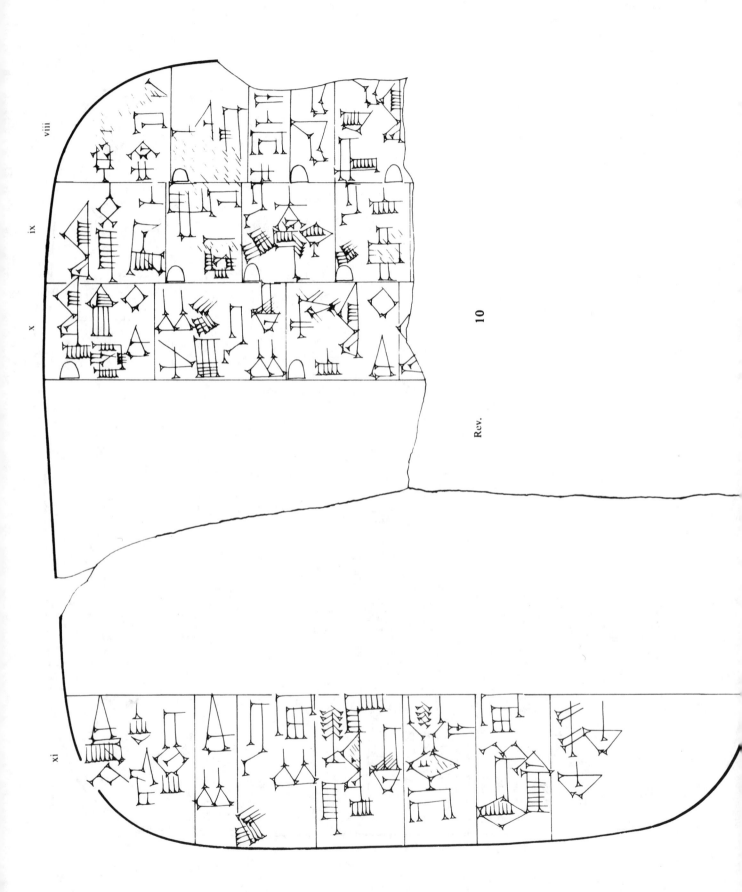

10

Rev.

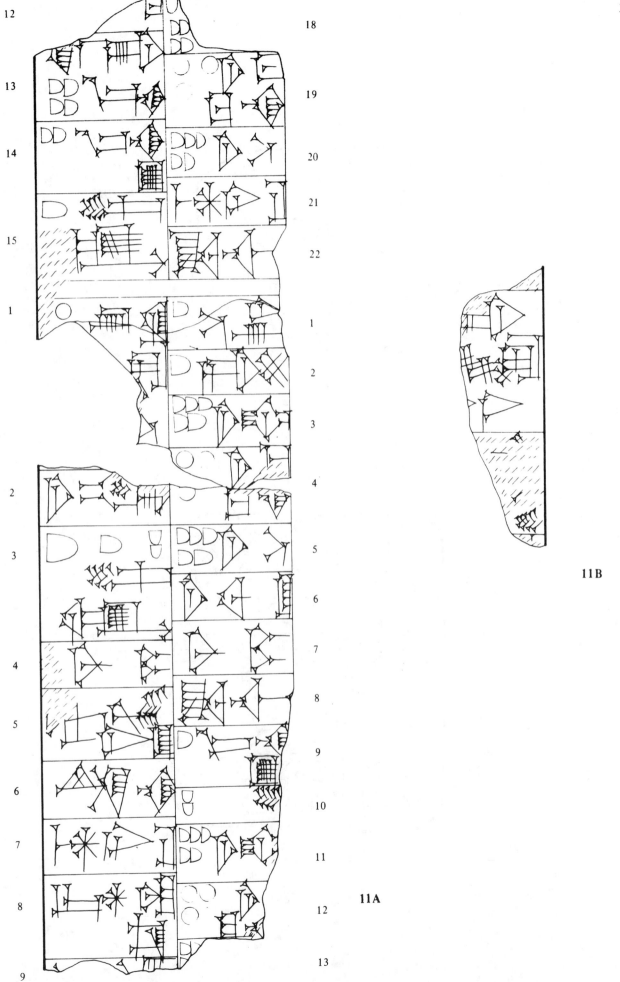

11A

11B

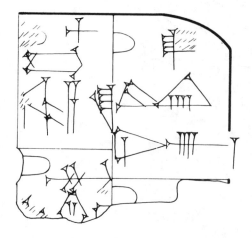

12

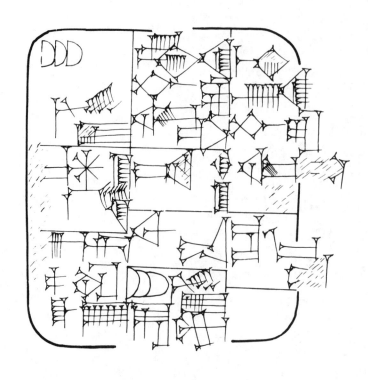

13

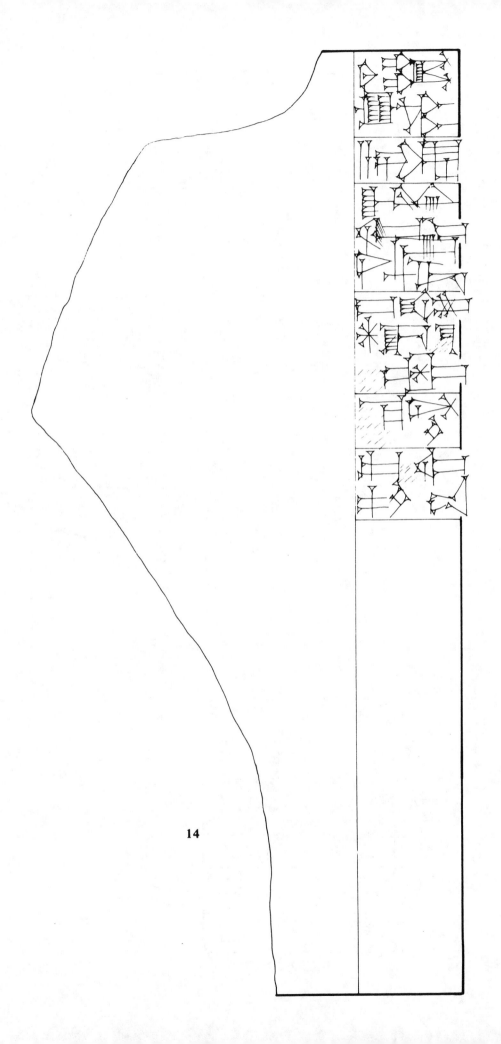

14

i   ii   iii   iv

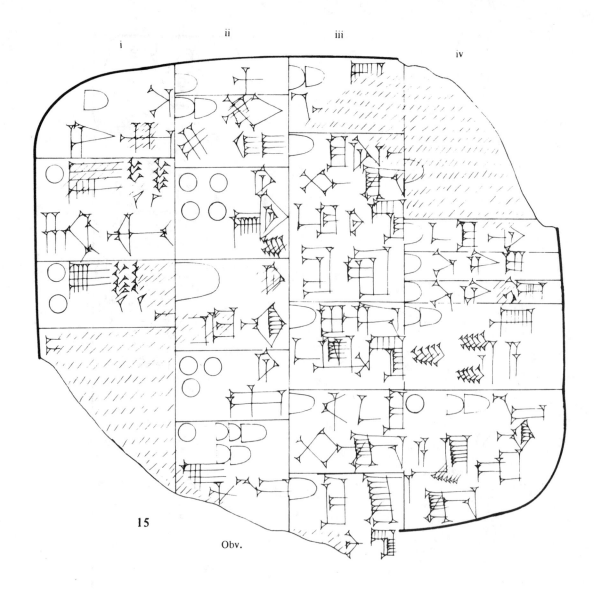

15

Obv.

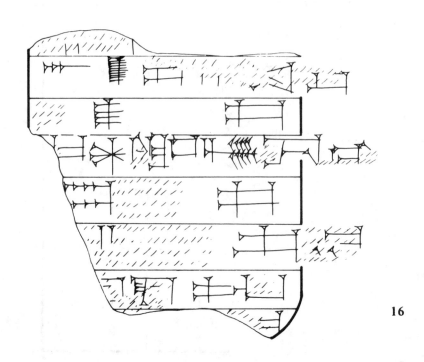

16

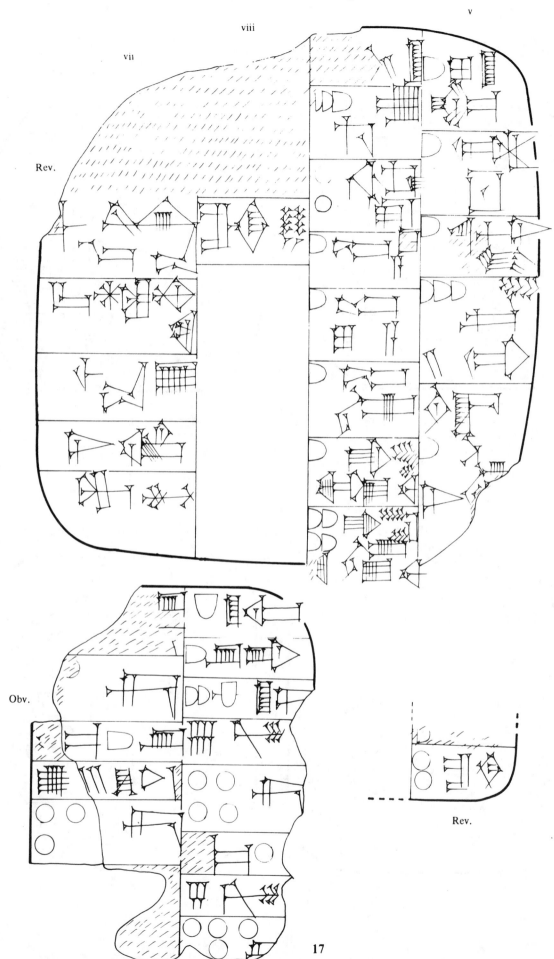

18

Obv.

Rev.

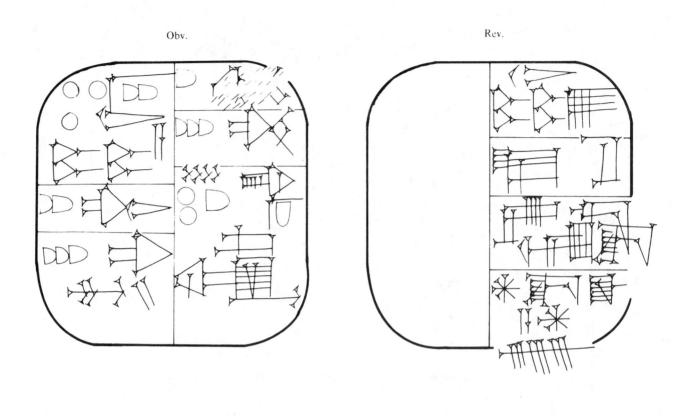

19

Obv.

Rev.

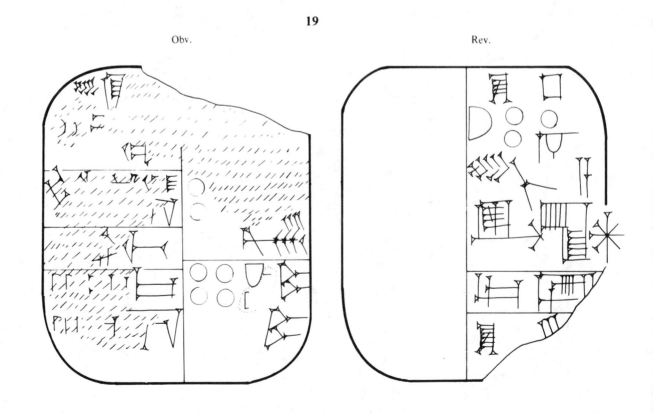

20

21

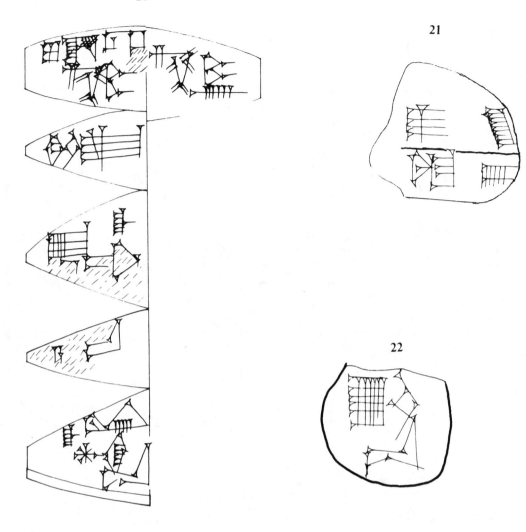

22

23

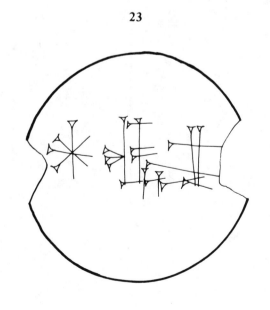

24

Obv.

Rev.

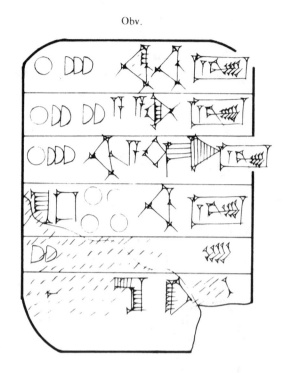
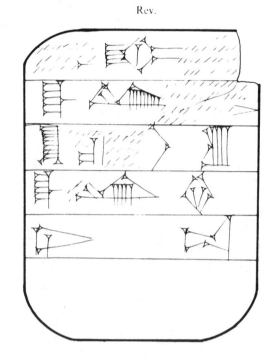

25

Obv.

Rev.

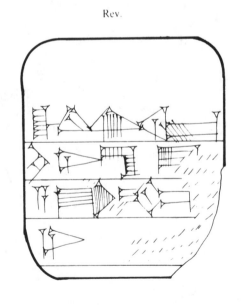

26

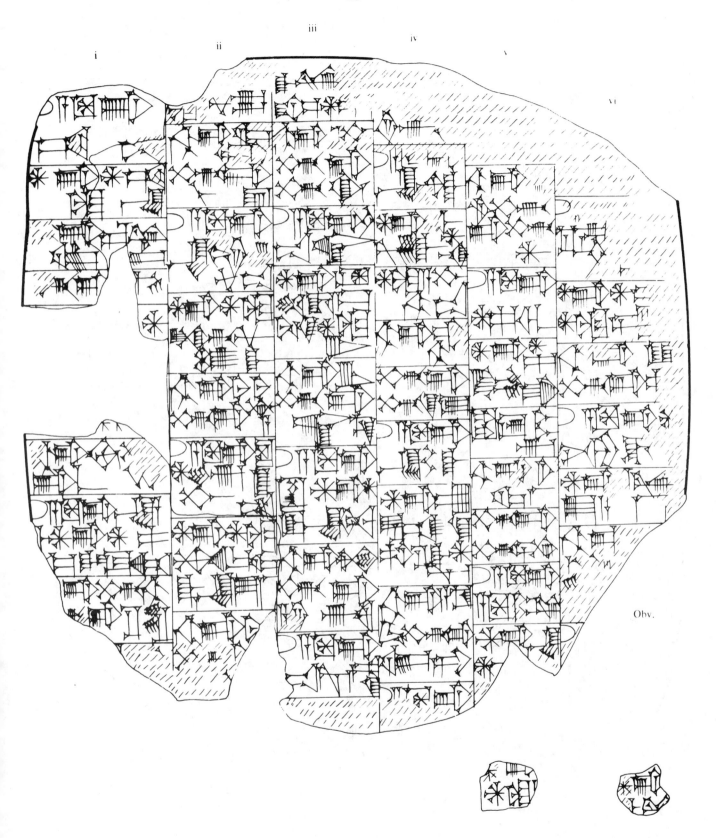

i   ii   iii   iv   v   vi

Obv.

Fragments

34

26

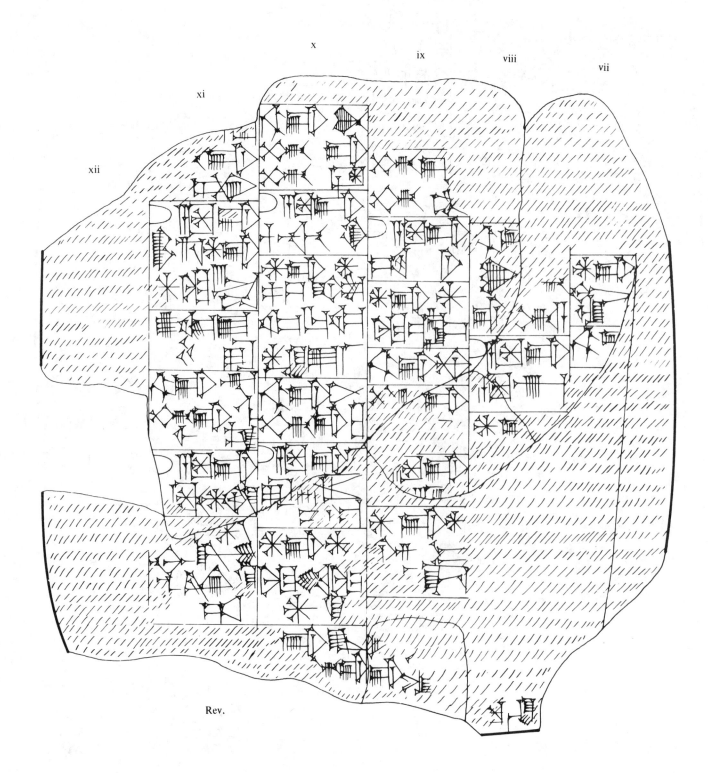

xii xi x ix viii vii

Rev.

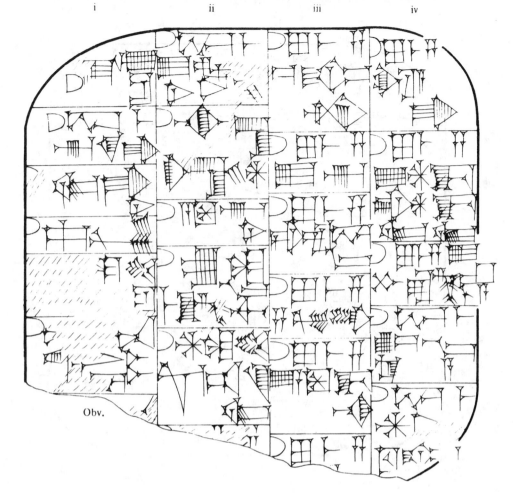

i　　ii　　iii　　iv

Obv.

27

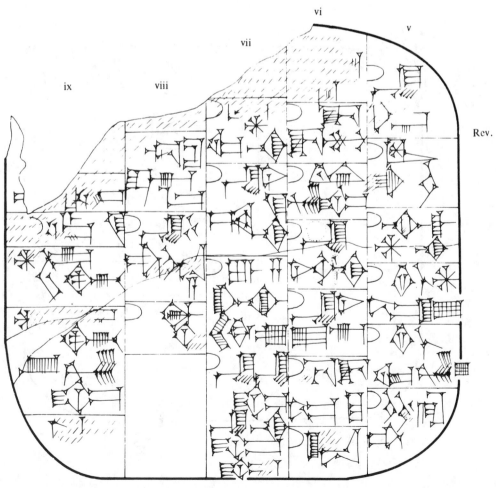

vi

vii

v

ix　　viii

Rev.

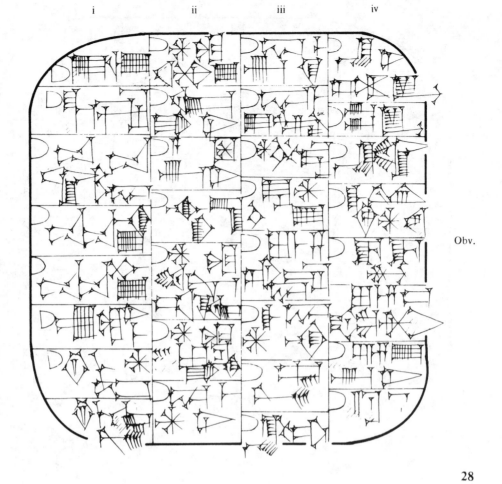

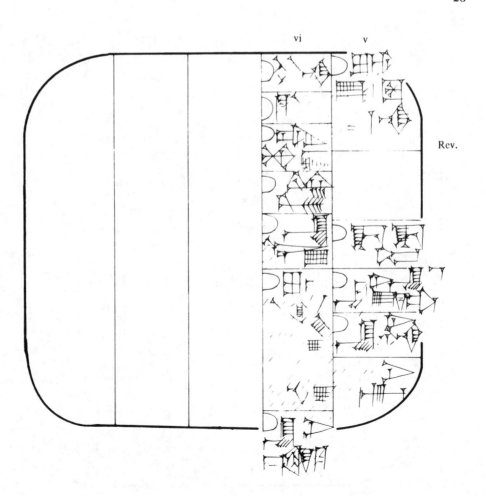

36

i ii iii iv

Obv.

28

vi v

Rev.

29

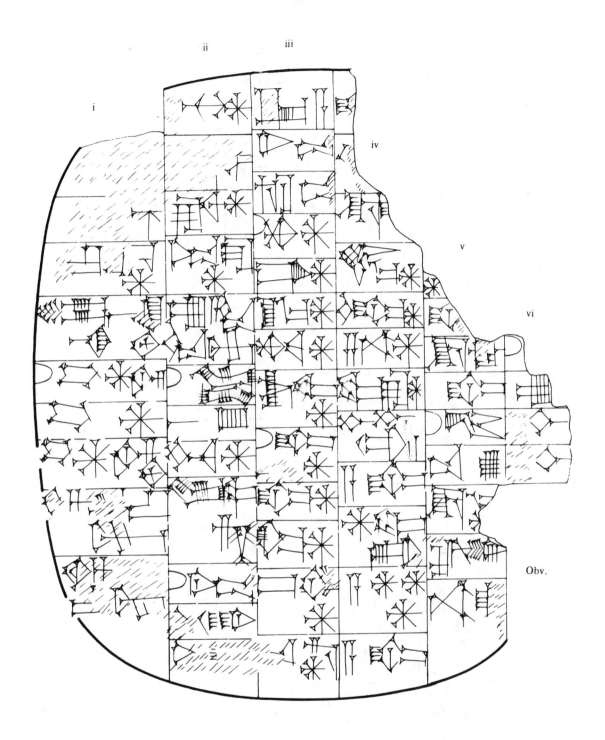

Obv.

Fragment

29

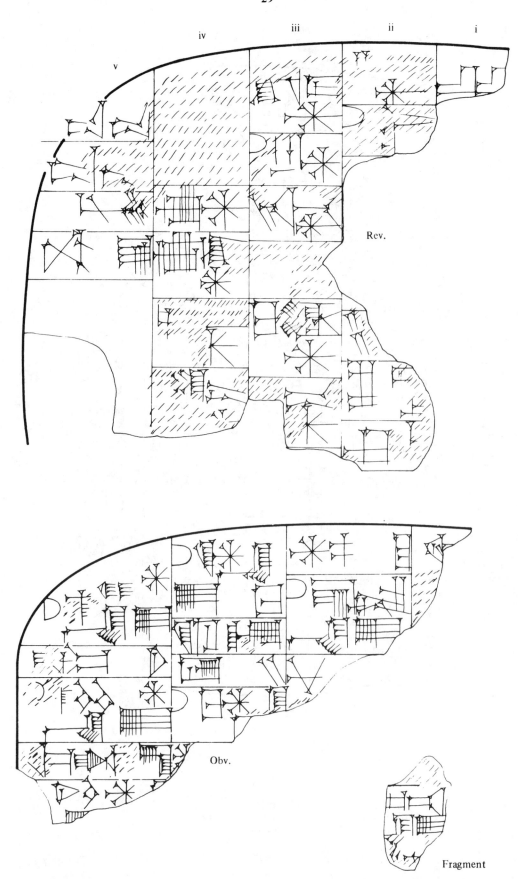

30

30

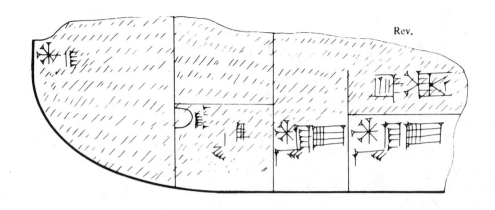

Rev.

31

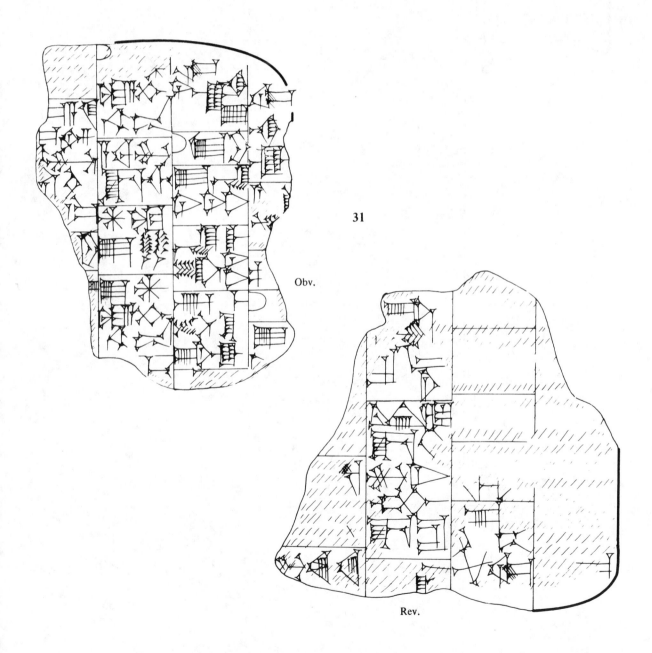

Obv.

Rev.

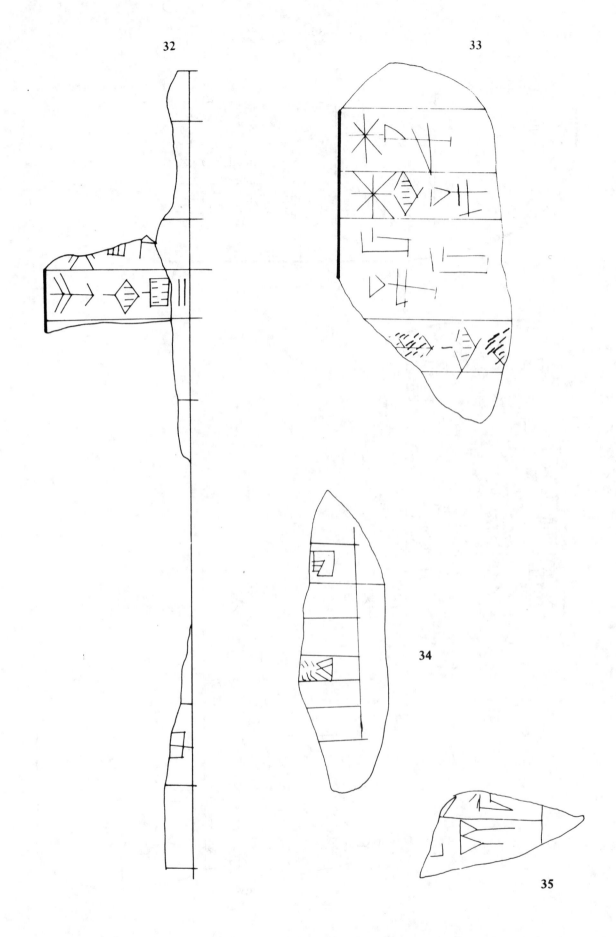

36

Obv.

Obv.

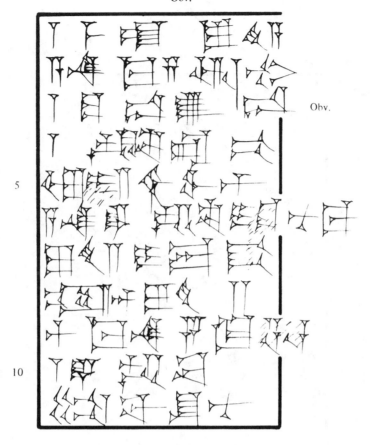

5

10

37

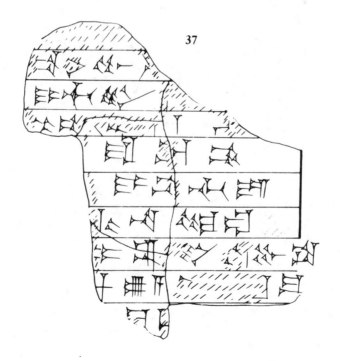

36

Rev.

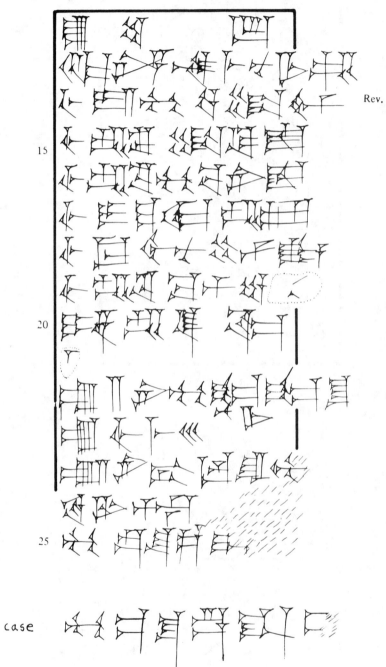

Rev.

15

20

25

case

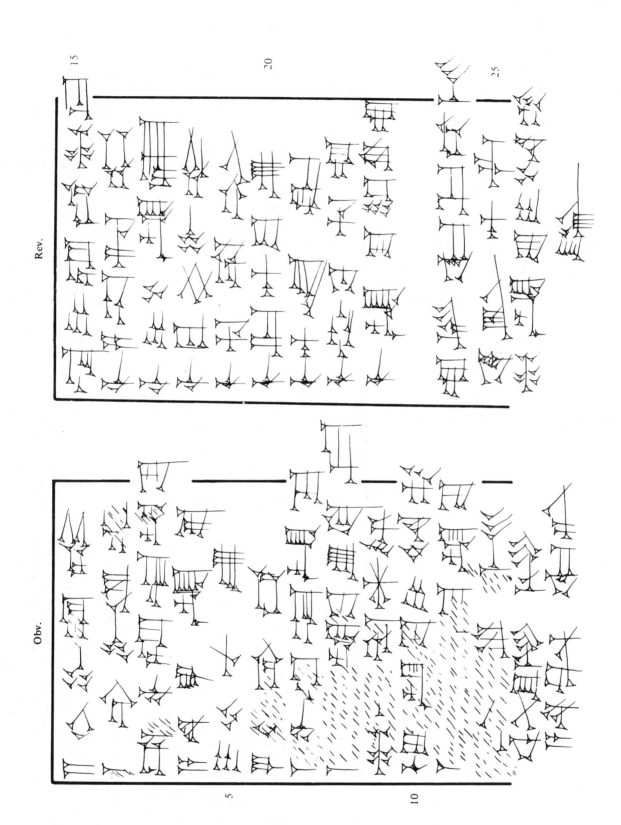

44

39A

Obv.   Rev.

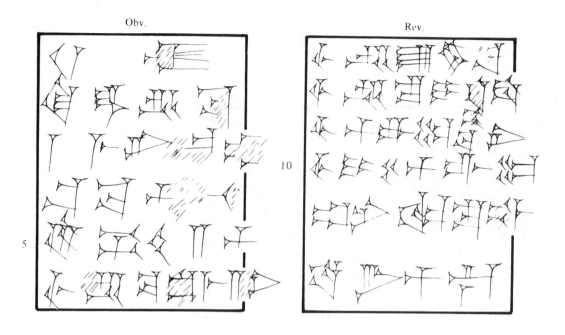

10

5

39B

Obv.   Rev.

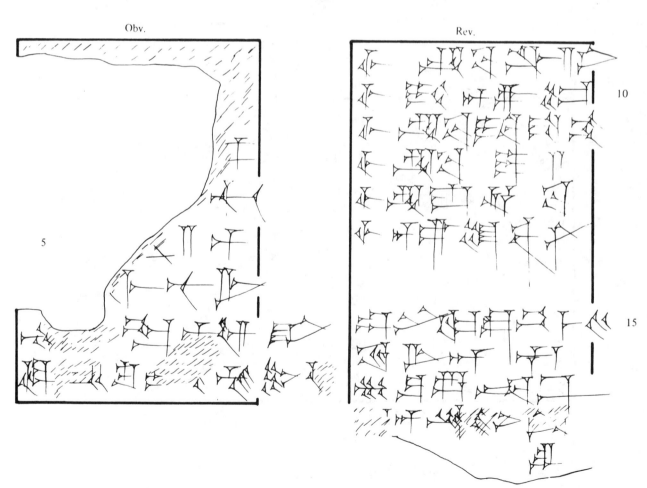

5

10

15

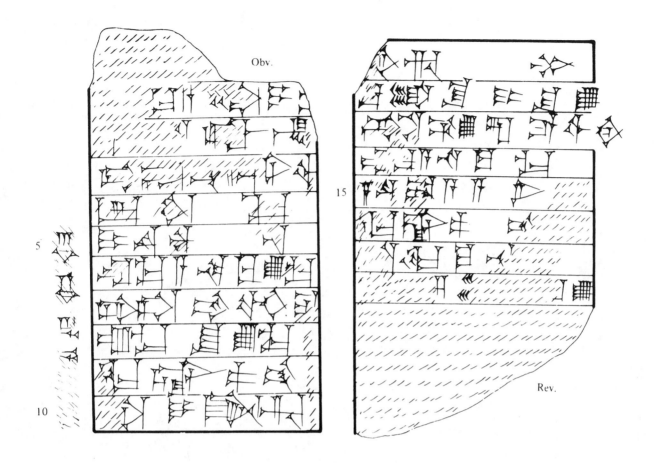

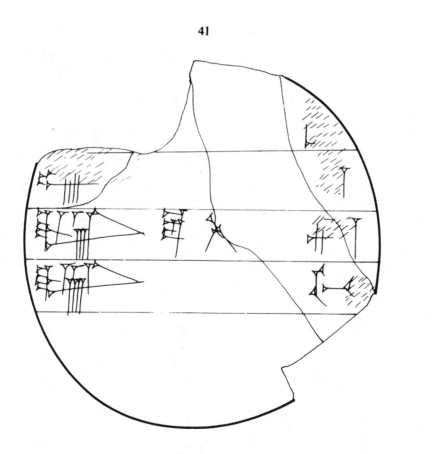

PLATES

Fig. 2

Seal impressions on the edge of the case of No. 36

Fig. 1

Seal impressions on the left edge of No. 36

Fig. 3

Seal impressions on the obverse of the case of No. 36

Fig. 4

Seal impressions on the left edge of No. 38